W9-DDL-180

The Vegetable Group

by Helen Frost

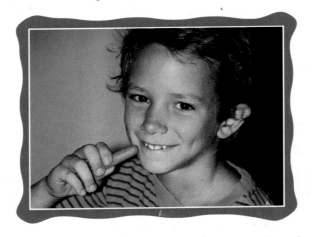

Consulting Editor: Gail Saunders-Smith, Ph.D.

Consultant: Linda Hathaway
Health Educator
McMillen Center for Health Education

Pebble Books

an imprint of Capstone Press
Mankato, Minnesota

Pebble Books are published by Capstone Press
151 Good Counsel Drive, P.O. Box 669, Mankato, Minnesota 56002
http://www.capstone-press.com

Copyright © 2000 Capstone Press. All rights reserved.
No part of this book may be reproduced without written permission
from the publisher. The publisher takes no responsibility for the use of any
of the materials or methods described in this book, nor for the products thereof.
Printed in the United States of America.

1 2 3 4 5 6 05 04 03 02 01 00

Library of Congress Cataloging-in-Publication Data
Frost, Helen, 1949–
    The vegetable group/by Helen Frost.
    p. cm.—(Food guide pyramid)
    Includes bibliographical references and index.
    Summary: Simple text and photographs present the foods that are part of the
vegetable group and their nutritional importance.
    ISBN 0-7368-0541-9
    1. Vegetables—Juvenile literature. 1. Nutrition—Juvenile literature.
[1. Vegetables. 2. Nutrition.] I. Title. II. Series.
TX391.F76   2000
613.2—dc21
                                                                    99-047742

Note to Parents and Teachers

The Food Guide Pyramid series supports national science standards related to physical health and nutrition. This book describes and illustrates the vegetable group. The photographs support early readers in understanding the text. The repetition of words and phrases helps early readers learn new words. This book also introduces early readers to subject-specific vocabulary words, which are defined in the Words to Know section. Early readers may need assistance to read some words and to use the Table of Contents, Words to Know, Read More, Internet Sites, and Index/Word List sections of the book.

Table of Contents

4

The food guide pyramid
shows the foods you
need to stay healthy.
The vegetable group is
near the bottom of the
food guide pyramid.

A vegetable is the part of a plant that people eat.

Corn is in the
vegetable group.

Broccoli is in the vegetable group.

Celery is in the
vegetable group.

Carrots are in the vegetable group.

Potatoes are in the
vegetable group.

Peas are in the
vegetable group.

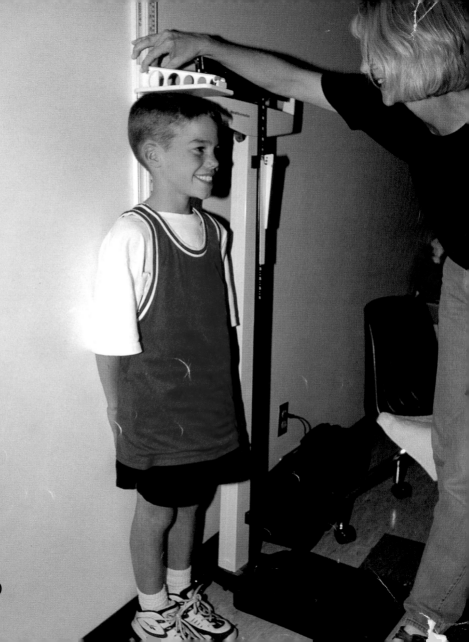

You need three to five
servings of vegetables
every day. Vegetables
help you grow and
stay healthy.

food guide pyramid—a triangle split into six areas to show the different foods people need; a pyramid is big at the bottom and small at the top; people need more food from the bottom of the food guide pyramid than from the top.

healthy—fit and well; vegetables have nutrients that help people stay healthy.

serving—a helping of food or drink; one serving from the vegetable group is 1/2 cup (125 ml) of chopped raw or cooked vegetables, 1 cup (250 ml) of raw leafy vegetables, or 3/4 cup (175 ml) of vegetable juice.

vegetable—the part of a plant that people eat; vegetables come from many parts of a plant; vegetables can be roots, stems, leaves, flowers, or seeds.

Read More

Frost, Helen. *Eating Right.* The Food Guide Pyramid. Mankato, Minn.: Pebble Books, 2000.

Kalbacken, Joan. *The Food Pyramid.* A True Book. New York: Children's Press, 1998.

Powell, Jillian. *Vegetables.* Everyone Eats. Austin, Texas: Raintree Steck-Vaughn, 1997.

Saunders-Smith, Gail. *Carrots.* Plants. Mankato, Minn.: Pebble Books, 1997.

Internet Sites

Food Guide Pyramid
http://kidshealth.org/kid/food/pyramid.html

Food Guide Pyramid Game
http://www.nppc.org/cgi-bin/pyramid

Just for Kids
http://www.dole5aday.com/menu/kids/menu.htm

Vegetables
http://www.nal.usda.gov:8001/py/pveg.htm

Index/Word List

broccoli, 11
carrots, 15
celery, 13
corn, 9
eat, 7
food guide pyramid, 5
foods, 5
grow, 21

healthy, 5, 21
peas, 19
plant, 7
potatoes, 17
servings, 21
vegetable, 7, 21
vegetable group, 5, 9,
    11, 13, 15, 17, 19

Word Count: 88
Early-Intervention Level: 8

Editorial Credits

Mari C. Schuh, editor; Heather Kindseth, cover designer; Sara A. Sinnard, illustrator;
    Kia Bielke, illustrator; Kimberly Danger, photo researcher

Photo Credits

David F. Clobes, 12
Gregg R. Andersen, cover, 6
Kim Stanton, 1
Matt Swinden, 20
Robert Finken/Index Stock Imagery, 14
Unicorn Stock Photos/Eric Berndt, 8
Visuals Unlimited/Mark S. Skalny, 10; W. J. Weber, 16; McCutcheon, 18